NATIONAL GEOGRAPHIC

T0045261

A Good Place to Live

Marvin Buckley

My town is a good place to live.

People keep my town clean.

This person cleans the streets.

This person takes away the trash.

This person cuts the grass in the park.

People keep my town safe.

police officer

This person directs traffic.

fire fighter

This person puts out fires.

This person fixes pipes under the road.

People help each other in my town.

This person helps us cross the street.

This person helps us find books to read.

This person helps sick people.

Yes, my town is a good place to live!